SEE ONE
DO ONE
TEACH ONE

12 LESSONS TO SUPPORT
GCSE ENGLISH

MARTIN FERGUSON

First published 2023

by John Catt Educational Ltd,
15 Riduna Park, Station Road,
Melton, Woodbridge IP12 1QT

Tel: +44 (0) 1394 389850
Email: enquiries@johncatt.com
Website: www.johncatt.com

ISBN: 978 1 915 261 32 8

Set and designed by John Catt Educational Limited

Contents

To my brilliant wife Máire – thank you for all your love, support and encouragement. You have all the best ideas!

Introduction

'I hear and I forget. I see and I remember. I do and I understand.' – Confucius

The concept for the series of lessons in this book came about after a discussion with my wife in relation to her work in surgical training and as a doctor. I first became aware of the phrase 'see one, do one, teach one' when she explained that it was used by medical personnel, particularly surgical trainees. Medical procedures are often taught by observation, participation and then progression towards independence. Around the same time, I was reading Tom Sherrington's *Rosenshine's Principles in Action* and the discussions around the practical application of the principles were becoming more prevalent in mainstream educational circles. Consequently, the idea to create a series of lessons around this concept was born and the name *See One, Do One, Teach One* was adopted.

'SODOTO' provides a series of 12 engaging lessons for GCSE English pupils, with some focus on the Northern Ireland CCEA specification. The lessons have been created for pupils of all abilities and are based on tried and tested methods within a classroom setting; they have a high success rate and have created a lesson planning template for myself and a form of routine for my pupils. Pupils learn through direct observation of each task and are guided carefully through each task often using a visualiser.

Having had the privilege of working within an all-ability setting for most of my career, I wanted to create a series of lessons that were practical, structured and that would also support NQTs in the early years of teaching exam classes. The early years of teaching can be a bit of a treadmill and perhaps this book could help those new teachers step on with more confidence. These lessons can also apply to any class or cohort that you see fit or can be used as a model or resource for CPD.

Each lesson can act as a springboard or can provide an opportunity to review and refresh your teaching approaches for GCSE English Language. Using *Rosenshine's Principles for Instruction*, I decided to primarily focus on direct instruction, scaffolding, live modelling and careful annotation.

There are also opportunities to act on feedback using extension tasks. I also wanted to embed an oracy skills element through the speaking and listening lesson and in the 'Teach One' section.

Pupils 'see' an example in action delivered by an expert; 'do' by completing a related task under the supervision of their teacher; and finally, they 'teach' each other by using carefully constructed questions for micro teaching or for paired and group discussion.

In the 'See One' part of the lesson, the class teacher will outline the task and discuss the model example to demystify the learning and break down the task appropriately. Obviously, there will be activated prior knowledge and reviewing of what they have learned beforehand. Narrating and talking through the task will prove beneficial and allows for pupils to ask questions or seek clarification. Again, you can modify the lesson to suit your cohort or use it as a template or form of repeated practice throughout the year to embed routines.

In the 'Do One' section, the scaffolds will help reinforce the knowledge and skills learned and will allow pupils to develop towards mastery. The model example can be displayed for the class as a point of reference to coincide with the scaffolds. This allows them to make the connection between what is expected in their answers and how they can merge this with their own thoughts and ideas. You can also convert those scaffolds into structure strips or separate learning resources.

'Teach One' is aimed at effectively 'closing the loop' using oracy and independent learning skills. It will allow pupils to engage with one another in loosely scripted and rich classroom discussion. One pupil becomes the learner and the other becomes the teacher. Many pupils view the front of a classroom as a sacred space or the floor suddenly becomes lava when you ask some of them to come forward, demonstrate to the class and share their thoughts and ideas. For the less assured pupils, you can see the blood drain from their face and the eyes begin to avoid direct contact when you are fishing for volunteers. With these lessons and the structures in place, hopefully it will help you to develop experts amongst peers and encourage participation and confidence.

If we embed this practice early then it becomes second nature and so does conversation, debate and meaningful discussion. This is the kind of classroom we all want and that is why the 'Teach One' section can act as a one-to-one resource for pupils, classroom assistants or teachers.

The lessons include a variation of the following:

- Material and tasks in small incremental steps.
- Models to explore, analyse and evaluate.
- Scaffolds that can be adapted or modified.
- Prompts and key terms to encourage 'rich talk'.
- Independent and guided practice.
- Opportunities for oracy development and peer discussion.
- Vocabulary development and awareness.

Often when we meet pupils at GCSE level, we don't have the time to take them back to basics while simultaneously teaching to an exam specification in a given time frame. The lessons and strategies included in this book are not a silver bullet, nor are they intended to be, but they will provide accessible strategies that can be developed over time by the class teacher alongside the pupil.

By using research informed practice and combining effective and powerful strategies, the overarching aim for all of us is to become more effective and responsive teachers. Therefore, John Hattie's effect sizes have been carefully considered alongside Rosenshine's principles so I was conscious of embedding both the principles and the effect sizes in areas such as: questioning [0.48], direct instruction [0.59], deliberate practice [0.79], discussion [0.82], and scaffolding [0.82][1]

Terms used above interpreted suggest:[2]

- An effect size of 0.5 is equivalent to a one grade leap at GCSE.
- An effect size of 1.0 is equivalent to a two-grade leap at GCSE.

---

1   Waack, S. (no date). Hattie Ranking: 252 Influences And Effect Sizes Related To Student Achievement. Retrieved from: bit.ly/3las4UE.

2   The Teachers Toolbox (no date). Professor John Hattie's Table of Effect Sizes. Retrieved from: www.teacherstoolbox.co.uk/effect-sizes/.

Supporting SEND pupils

'The evidence tells us that teachers should instead prioritise familiar but powerful strategies, like scaffolding and explicit instruction, to support their pupils with SEND.'[3] – Professor Becky Francis

For SEND pupils, the lessons in this book might also provide opportunities for you to fine tune them for your own context. SEND pupils feel safe when there is a consistent and predictable routine in place, be that behaviour based in terms of preparing for learning beforehand or in terms of delivery of content during the lesson. Combining the two approaches can be very potent as routines can encourage positive behaviour whereas inconsistency causes anxiety and frustration.

Well-established routines can help to reduce a pupil's anxiety as they can be confident in knowing what will happen next, how people around them will behave and what they will need to do to complete their task. Here are some things you can do to support SEND pupils:

- Keep instructions clear and concise.
- Verbalise your thought process while modelling activities.
- Give children an opportunity to repeat instructions back to you or do a joint walkthrough.
- Deploy classroom assistants to effectively facilitate learning using the lessons or 'Teach One' sheet.
- Organise work for learners with SEND in smaller chunks with plenty of opportunities for revisiting and over learning – edit the lessons where you see fit and note where the pinch points are during your lessons.
- Incorporate flexible grouping – do not always group children with similar SEND together.
- Create groups or 'talk partners' to review the learning.
- Be consistent when applying rules and remind and rehearse them regularly .

---

3   Education Endowment Foundation (2020). Special Educational Needs In Mainstream Schools: Guidance Report, bit.ly/3IqkcWT.

Each lesson is purposeful, structured and systematic which I hope will provide you with practical and tangible resources that can be taken directly from this book and into your classroom. I hope that it helps lighten the load of the heavy lifting that often occurs at GCSE level and perhaps even encourage you to review your own lesson structures and approaches elsewhere in your teaching such as Key Stage 3.

Our English department motto is from the great Irish poet and scholar Seamus Heaney and is something that has stuck with me throughout my career: 'If you have the words, there's always a chance that you'll find the way'. Hopefully this series of lessons will give pupils the words so that they have the chance to find their confidence and achieve success along the way.

Sentence structure and variation

Prerequisites or core knowledge recap

- Simple, compound, and complex sentences
- Use of basic punctuation
- Awareness of punctuation and its effect

Suggestion: Use highlighters to code the writing in the following passages.

Example 1: Here is a piece of writing that lacks sentence variety.

I woke up. The moon was shining into my room. It was raining outside, and I could hear it. I lay still and listened to the rain. I turned on my phone to check the time. It was very late. I walked to the window and closed the curtains. Then I got back into my bed.

Example 2: What improvements has the writer made?

I woke up. The moonlight was shining through the curtains. The rain was hitting the window and was making a loud noise. I lay still and listened. I leaned across the bed and turned on my phone. It was the early hours of the morning. I walked towards the window. I closed the curtains. I got back into my bed.

Example 3: What has the writer done to make this more interesting?

I opened my eyes to the light of the moon that was beaming through the heavy curtains. The rain was relentlessly striking the window, breaking the night-time silence. Leaning across the bed, I turned on my phone and checked the time; it was 2:30am. I padded across the wooden floor towards the large window. Delicately, I closed the curtains to block out the remaining light. I carefully crawled back into my warm bed, gently shutting my eyes.

Read the following piece aloud to the class or with the class.

There is a video to accompany it. Then ask the class to answer the following question:

1. What do you think the writer is trying to say?
2. What are they trying to tell us about writing and sentences?
3. Write down three to five things this writer does that makes this piece interesting.

> This sentence has five words. Here are five more words. Five-word sentences are fine. But several together become monotonous. Listen to what is happening. The writing is getting boring. The sound of it drones. It's like a stuck record. The ear demands some variety.
>
> Now listen. I vary the sentence length, and I create music. Music. The writing sings. It has a pleasant rhythm, a lilt, a harmony. I use short sentences. And I use sentences of medium length. And sometimes when I am certain the reader is rested, I will engage him with a sentence of considerable length, a sentence that burns with energy and builds with all the impetus of a crescendo, the roll of the drums, the crash of the cymbals—sounds that say listen to this, it is important.
>
> So write with a combination of short, medium, and long sentences. Create a sound that pleases the reader's ear. Don't just write words. Write music.

Figure 1: Aerogramme Writers' Studio (2014) This Sentence Has Five Words: A Lesson From Gary Provost On Varying Sentence Length, [online] 5 August. Retrieved from: bit.ly/3I06Hyl.

Dual coding

_____ = simple

_____ + _____ = compound

_____, _____ = complex

1. *Do you agree or disagree with what the writer is saying about sentences?*
2. *What language features can you spot in this piece of writing?*
3. *How does this make you think about your own writing?*

Now it's your turn!

Remember to use your notes to guide you.

Take your time and begin with the basics and then build your writing gradually.

1. Select *one* of the following or make up your own:

- Going to school in the morning   [I was late…]
- Lying on a tropical beach whilst on holiday   [I was on the beach…]
- Getting ready to go to a party or event   [I was excited…]

Begin with the basics

Example 1: Write a simple description of your chosen topic or event

_____

_____

_____

_____

Example 2: Can you improve your writing?

_____

_____

_____

_____

Example 3: Can you add more detail?

_____

_____

_____

_____

_____

_____

_____

In your pairs, decide who will be the **teacher** and who will be the **learner**.
You will use your notes to take the learner through the process step by step.

Teacher: _____ **Learner:** _____

Instructions: Take your time going through each stage.

1. Ask the learner to tell you what simple, compound and complex sentences are. You can prompt or remind them if they forget or need reminded.

2. Recap on what is on your 'See One' sheet and, in your own words, explain it to the learner. Ask the learner to briefly explain back to you again.

3. Now take the learner through your own 'Do One' example and explain to them how you have developed your writing.

4. Ask the learner to select examples of the different types of sentences in your own examples and spot the differences.

5. Now, ask the learner to pick a scenario or idea that they will use for their writing. Your teacher may put some more examples on the board for you to choose from.

6. Ask the learner to put the basic details of their paragraph in order. You can use the examples to help you.

7. This time, ask them to expand their ideas in a similar way to the second example by adding slightly more detail.

Final challenge: Working together now, try and write a final paragraph. Support one another and add in any ideas you think will make the writing more interesting.

Oracy task: Can you can present your final paragraph to the class and show them how you got there?

Varying sentence openers

Openers are the key to starting a good sentence and add variety to your writing. They also help demonstrate that you can control your writing while, at the same time, adding action and variety can engage the reader.

Without them, you can often get stuck using 'I', 'he/she', or the character's name. It is also very common for a story or recount to include too many examples of 'then' at the beginning of the sentence.

Openers give variety, although they can make a piece of writing seem over the top if used for every sentence, so it is important to use them effectively. It is good to be exposed to as many sentence openers as often as possible. As you become more confident with your openers, you can also begin to be more selective in your choices and vocabulary.

Do you use 'then' too often? This simple exercise that follows will help you to replace the word 'then' in your writing and will develop your awareness of different ways of starting a sentence. It will also help you to paragraph your writing or add logical sequencing.

Here are some examples for you to read, can you write your own version beneath each sentence using the opener in bold?

After the storm, the villagers decided to rebuild their homes.

Once in a while, I would sit outside and gaze at the stars.

Beneath the murky water, the kraken waited for the ship to pass.

With a trembling hand, the pupil opened the door to the headmaster's office.

At the top of the cliff, there appeared to be a ghostly figure.

As quick as a flash, the bullet whizzed past his ear at the parapet.

DO

Now it's your turn!

Remember to use your notes to guide you.

Take your time and begin with basic or familiar openers and then add more detail.

Modelled example

Although it was late at night, Ollie had to remain alert as he was on sentry duty. At around 4am, a ghostly blanket of fog began to hover over the ground. He yearned for the morning sunrise. Slowly, one by one, the bodies of the soldiers were revealed as the fog lifted. With a shaking hand, he gently lifted his rifle and peered down his scope in search of survivors.

1. Select three openers from the boxes below and extend the sentence using your own ideas.

2. Select three openers and try to write three paragraphs – can you connect them?

3. Write a short story and use a variety of sentence openers from the following boxes or use one of the sentences to extend a story or idea. You can use them as building blocks or triggers. Remember to include a variety of sentences or use the modelled example above.

If you have a dice or a way of colouring or labelling the boxes, you can turn this activity into a challenge or game!	**Where?** At the front of the house, he stopped and wondered ... Next to the lake, there was a bench ...	**When?** By dawn, the light began to ... At 6pm, on a cold October evening ...
How? Full of confusion, Tom ran off. Not caring at all, the toddler kicked the door.	**-ing** Strolling down the corridor, ... Breathing quietly, ... Inspecting the classroom, ...	**-ed** Horrified, the boy ... Filled with excitement, ... Stunned in silence, ...
Adverb Slowly, the creature ... Carefully, he moved ... Frantically, she searched ...	**Connective** Although it was late at night, ... Despite the thick fog, she was able to ...	**Simile** Quiet as a mouse, the robber ... Like a charging bull, he ...

 **TEACH**   Varying sentence openers

In your pairs, decide who will be the **teacher** and who will be the **learner**.
You will use your notes to take the learner through the process step by step.

1. Ask the learner the following questions:

   What is an **adverb**? Give me three examples of an adverb.

   What is a **fronted adverbial**? Give me three examples of a fronted adverbial.

   Can you give **three reasons** why we should use a variety of sentence openers?

   If they need prompting, you can help them to recall what they have learned and/or correct them using your own sheet.

2. Now take the learner through your '**Do One**' example and explain to them how you have developed your writing using the openers you have selected.

3. Ask the learner if the task was challenging or straightforward. Ask them what difficulties they encountered and if this exercise could help their writing.

4. Ask the learner to select examples from their piece of writing and explain their reasons for choosing each opener and how it helped to develop their writing.

5. Now, write down three or more sentence openers for the learner, leaving a few lines below each one, and ask them to extend each sentence. They can be related or they can be individual sentences.

   Final challenge: Working together now, create a bank of ten different openers. Share or swap them with another pair in the class and challenge them to write a short story or piece of writing.

   Oracy task: Can you can present your final pieces of writing by reading them to the class or mix them together and read someone else's aloud?

Cross-curricular writing challenge

Prerequisites or resources

- Various subject word banks made available
- Common Latin or Greek roots or suffixes and prefixes
- Whiteboards and markers

Word Bank A

- meandered
- perimeter
- atrium
- absorb
- exhale
- hygiene
- prepare
- function
- multiple

- range
- average
- password
- document
- positive
- fraction
- rhythm
- scale
- harmony

- creation
- eternal
- faith
- invasion
- motive
- siege
- sketch

Task 1: Can you group the words above in relation to the subject that they might belong to? Can they have more than one meaning?

Task 2: Can you select five words and use them in a sentence?

SEE

Cross-curricular writing challenge

Read the following example and highlight the cross curricular words that the writer has used.

> *Within a fraction of a second, we knew that the scale of what we had done would go down in history. The rhythm of daily life, routine and relative harmony within the prison turned to immediate chaos. There was an invasion of multiple prison officers, guard dogs and army personnel.*
>
> *We were under siege.*
>
> *Luckily, we had prepared some maps and sketches of the tunnel system in the old document room next to the library. The narrow tunnels meandered beneath the atrium but we had to get to the pump room to access them. I had faith that we would make it out alive. I was barely able to function in here for six months, never mind for the rest of my life. The poor hygiene, the confined space, not to mention the tasteless slop they called food, were motive enough.*
>
> *I had to remain positive, otherwise I was facing an eternity behind bars!*
> *Once we get to the perimeter fence it will finally be all over.*
>
> *Freedom.*

Now it's your turn!

Using **one** of the word banks below, write your own creative story using as many words as you can.

You can time yourself or your class or ask your teacher to have a go!

Word Bank A

- meandered
- perimeter
- atrium
- absorb
- exhale
- hygiene
- prepare
- function
- multiple

- range
- average
- password
- document
- positive
- fraction
- rhythm
- scale
- harmony

- creation
- eternal
- faith
- invasion
- motive
- siege
- sketch

Word Bank B

- erupted
- measure
- calculate
- experiment
- beaker
- cloud
- mouse
- timeline

- evidence
- battle
- conquer
- story
- character
- discussion
- debate
- listen

- prayer
- creation
- eternal
- faith
- shade
- motive
- spectrum
- magnetic

Your task is to teach your partner new words related to the subjects or topics you have learned in school. Good luck!

1. Create a grid using **key terms** or words from other subjects.

   You can use your word bank that your teacher has given you.

2. Explain the **meaning** of each word that you have used to your partner and how it is connected to each subject.

3. Exchange grids with your partner and attempt to write your own short story using the words they have given you.

4. Set a timer or ask your teacher to set one and begin the writing challenge – you can do it without a timer if you prefer.

   You can add -*ing*, -*ed*, or shorten the word if you wish.

   How many have you used and have you used them correctly?

5. Read each other's pieces of writing and tick off each word as it appears. You can **allocate points** for each word in the grid in terms of difficulty. Share the best examples with the class.

1 point – familiar words	**2 points** – scientific words
3 points – words with three syllables	**4 points** – originality or flair

'Word gaps': crafting, drafting and editing

Prerequisites, core knowledge or resources

- Sentence structure and variation recap
- Sentence openers recap
- Whiteboards and marker pens to craft and draft

Task 1: Read the following example of a personal writing first draft by a pupil.

What are your thoughts and opinions on this piece of writing? Could you improve it?

How would you improve it and what would you change, remove, or add?

> I walked to the school bus stop. It was a hot day, and my uniform was making me sweat, and my bag was hurting my back. The bus arrived and I got on with the rest of the pupils from my school. The bus was cramped, hot and uncomfortable. The windows were shut, and it was overcrowded. I was stuck beside the window with an older pupil who didn't speak to me. I looked out the window and began to daydream about the summer. I had one week left of exams and then I was free.

The following is an example of how we use 'word gaps' or opportunities to edit our writing to enhance the language and its overall appeal. Imagine that 'word gaps' are like adding smaller building blocks to strengthen your writing.

The pupil has used what they have learned about sentence variation and sentence openers to identify and develop areas for improvement.

> *I walked to the school bus stop. It was a hot day, and my uniform was making me sweat _____, and my bag was hurting my back. _____ the bus arrived, and I got on with the rest of the pupils from my school. The bus was cramped, hot and uncomfortable. The windows were shut, and it was overcrowded. I was stuck between the window with an older pupil who didn't speak to me. I looked out the window and began to daydream about the summer. I had one week left of exams, then I was free.*

This is the final crafted, drafted and edited piece:

> *Trudging up the hill, I could see the school bus stop on the **horizon**.*
> *It was a scorching hot day, and I began to **fester** and sweat **profusely** in my uniform. My bag was hanging like a monkey on my back. Eventually the rattly red bus arrived. Reluctantly, I boarded with the rest of the herd. The bus was like sitting in a **furnace**. The windows were sealed shut, and it was **teeming** with screenagers. I was trapped between the window and a **surly** sixth year who ignored my very existence. Gazing out the window, I drifted into a daydream about summer. Freedom was only a week away.*

Follow up task: Can you identify and explain any specific word choices, sentence openers or language techniques that this pupil has used?

Now it's your turn!

Remember to use your notes to guide you.

Take your time and begin with the basics and then build your writing gradually.

Writing task: Improve this pupil's writing below by identifying the 'word gaps' or opportunities to enhance their descriptive writing.

- **Read** the extract at least twice before you begin to think about changes.
- **Identify** where you could make improvements either using a highlighter or your own colour code.
- **Annotate and label** the piece of writing with your suggestions and ideas. Remember you can remove parts of the writing below as well. Do not be afraid to make changes in terms of basic vocabulary.
- **Redraft** the piece of writing by including your suggestions and improvements.
- **Proofread** and check that spelling, punctuation, and grammar are correct throughout.

It was a summer's evening, and the skies were clear and blue. It was perfect weather for an outdoor concert. There were crowds of people walking towards the park and they were singing and dancing. We were excited to get there early and get a good spot so we could see the performance. We joined the queue and handed over our tickets and walked in.

We were hungry after our journey in the car, so we decided to get some food from the food van. There was a good selection of food to choose from. The atmosphere and the excitement were building as it got darker and the concert lights began to light up the park. We found a good place to stand. Then the music began to play through the large speakers at the front and the lights began to flash. We had been waiting for this moment for a long time and it was finally here.

In your pairs, decide who will be the **teacher** and who will be the **learner**.
You will use your notes to take the learner through the process step by step.

1. Ask the learner the following questions:

    What are '**word gaps**' and how can they be used to improve our writing?

    What is a **sentence opener** and why do we use them?

    Can you give me three examples of sentence openers?

    If they need prompted, you can help them to recall what they have learned and/or correct them using your own sheet.

2. Now take the learner through your '**Do One**' example and explain to them how you have developed your writing using the 'word gaps' approach. Ask them to read it to you.

3. Ask the learner if they found the writing task challenging or straightforward. Ask them what difficulties they encountered and if this exercise has helped their understanding of writing.

4. Ask the learner to select examples from their piece of writing and explain their reasons for selecting and changing parts of the original draft, and how it has helped to make their writing more interesting.

5. **Final challenge**: Select one of the following scenarios and, in your pairs, try to write a joint piece of writing using what you have learned.

Going on holiday	Playing a sport	Celebrating an event

    Gather some ideas and draft it first then begin to break it down and decide how you could enhance each sentence. Try and keep it to 10-12 lines so that it remains focused and concise.

    Oracy task: Can you can present your final pieces of writing by reading them to the class or swap and share with another group?

Instead of ...

Prerequisites, core knowledge or resources
- Spend some time discussing synonyms
- Thesauri and dictionaries to gather ideas or words
- Whiteboards and marker pens to check prior vocabulary

Task 1: Write out as many different words you can think of for the verb '**looked**'.

Below are a series of synonyms for the verb 'looked'.

Drama based activity: In your pairs, use the word bank below to act out the various forms of the verb 'looked'.

inspected	noticed	examined	scouted	surveyed
focused	glanced	gazed	peeked	studied

Task 2: Using a mini whiteboard, select a word from the word bank above and write it in the centre.

Task 3: Now write down words that you think could be linked or associated with the word of your choice. An example has been done for you:

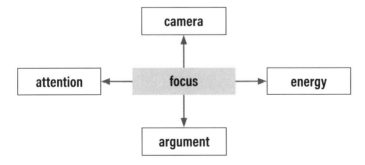

29

SEE Instead of ...

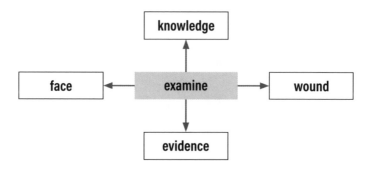

Follow-up task: Look up the word 'antonym' and ask the class to research the antonyms for the word 'looked' and complete the same exercise.

Now it's your turn!

We have completed a word association exercise to warm up our vocabulary muscles. Complete the exercise below to extend your vocabulary and use your own ideas to write your own sentences.

Using the word bank, fill in the sentences using the synonyms for the word 'looked'. Explain why you have chosen a particular word for each sentence, and why you think it is suitable.

1. The man _____ out the window of the bus.
2. The doctor _____ the patient's broken arm.
3. The bird _____ for mealworms in the garden.
4. The cat _____ over the fence.
5. Aslan _____ the land before making his way to the stone table.
6. The baseball player _____ on the speeding baseball.
7. She _____ at the stars in the night sky and noticed a strange object.
8. He _____ the portrait on the museum wall.
9. They _____ there was a sale on and decided to go into the shop.
10. The head teacher _____ their uniforms as they entered the school building.

inspected	noticed	examined	scouted	surveyed
focused	glanced	gazed	peeked	studied

Follow-up tasks:

1. Can you write ten of your own sentences for each of the words in the word bank?
2. Can you add *-ing* to any of the words in the word bank, and use them to change the sentence openings or create new ones?

In your pairs, decide who will be the **teacher** and who will be the **learner**.
You will use your notes to take the learner through the process step by step.

Other ways to say 'said'		
yelled	ranted	replied
announced	exclaimed	remarked
murmured	growled	declared
complained	boasted	sobbed
yawned	explained	whispered
barked	responded	groaned

Other ways to say _____		

1. Ask the learner to define the following words: adjective, verb, synonym and antonym.

2. Using the first table above, act out the words listed. You can do it in pairs taking one word each.

3. Using the table above, ask the learner to create a series of word association diagrams like the one you completed during the lesson. You can use a mini whiteboard.

4. Whilst they are completing the first step, construct ten sentences for the learner and ask them to fill in the gaps using the words from the word bank. Ask them to explain **why** they chose each word for each sentence.

5. Ask the learner to select another verb and make their own table using the example to guide them. For example, you could write for 'laughed' or 'walked'.

6. Write a short story using one of the opening sentences:

    'We arrived at the abandoned house…' or

    'Three of us. We were the only ones left on the island…'

    Include as many new action verbs as you can to enhance it. You can draft it together first and then replace the basic words with the new words you have learned.

Persuasive writing

Prerequisites, core knowledge or resources
- Define persuasion and discuss examples
- Recap persuasive devices and parts of speech
- Recap connectives and discursive markers

Pupil example:

Fellow screenagers, have you ever wondered what the world would look like without social media? Imagine having a good night's sleep without having to stop off for that energy drink on the way to school. Imagine being able to leave the house feeling good about yourself. Imagine talking to each other at the bus stop instead of staring at your phone.

It isn't that difficult to imagine, is it? To begin with, we need to free ourselves from the shackles of comments, likes and followers. We want to be free from the eyes of the world that are always ready to judge us at every turn. We want to live in a world without having to worry about what other people think of us and where we can be our true selves – that, my friends, is the dream!

In my opinion, social media is like a virus. It learns from us, evolves with our behaviours, and thrives on our very existence – and the one thing it takes for free? Our time! It robs us of our dignity, our individuality and worst of all our freedom. But why do we allow it to do so? Surely, we are in control? We have the power to defeat it, but why do we keep returning to this artificial world that thrives on fakery, fickle people and fabricated lifestyles? I will tell you why – because we are addicted!

Furthermore, social media is always available 24 hours a day, seven days a week, 365 days a year. It never sleeps (just like us). According to one report, the average teenager spends three hours on social media every single day – that is outrageous! So why is this important? Well, lack of sleep can lead to obesity, illness and poor grades in school. This means it is not only taking away our time but our health, our education and our future!

To conclude, I believe that we need to break these bad habits and take our lives back. How do we do that? I hear you ask. Well, it is very simple – make a choice every day to take time out, read a book, visit a family member or play sports. Instead of having our heads in our phones, we need to look up and see the real world around us. We only get one life, so we need to start living it through our friends and family – not through our screens!

Follow-up task: Label the language devices and discuss the impact they have on the audience.

Now it's your turn!
Remember to use your notes to guide you.
Take your time and begin with the basics and then build your writing gradually. Plan first then write!

Task 1: Discuss the issues that affect the lives of teenagers or list some topics that you think a teenage audience would be interested in.

Task 2: Construct your short speech using the example you have read and use the writing frame provided (you can work in pairs if you wish).

Introduction: You must address or 'hook' your reader or audience:

Fellow classmates...   *Have you ever...?*

Many people seem to think that...   *Imagine, for one minute, ...*

Include you/us/we or a rhetorical question:

We/You all know that...

Do you ever feel like...?

Are you fed up with...?

How could we deny that ...?

Don't get me wrong, ...

Emotive language:

Could you sum up how it makes you feel using a rule of three?

Using connectives to add structure:

To begin with, ...	*Firstly ...*	*Apart from ...*
In my opinion, ...	*Secondly ...*	*On the other hand ...*
Furthermore, ...	*Thirdly ...*	*However ...*

Endings should include a call to action or imperative:

To conclude, I believe that we need to ...

So, I leave you with this final thought, ...

DO

Bonus: Could you include any of the alliterative phrases below in your writing?

...deeply disturbing...	...simply shocking...	...mass misery...	...teenage troubles...
...picture perfect...	...incredibly interesting...	...difficult days...	...simple steps...
...terrible tragedy...	...bold and brave...	...fragile future...	...creating chaos...

In your pairs, decide who will be the **teacher** and who will be the **learner**. You will use your notes to guide the learner through the process step by step.

Ask the learner the following questions:

1. What does the word **persuade** mean?

   Can you give me **examples** of when persuasion is used?

   Can you name **five techniques** used in persuasive writing?

   Can you tell me **five connectives** or discursive markers?

2. Give the learner a topic from the list that you made earlier.

   Ask them to write down some ideas for their speech or persuasive essay. They can also read over your example or the first one.

3. Ask them to order their ideas (perhaps labelling them in order of importance) and decide which one they will use for their first, second and third paragraphs. Write them in bullet point order.

4. Using the writing frame, begin to write the first paragraph and guide the learner with the scaffold provided. Remind them that the introduction must hook or engage the reader.

5. Ask the learner to read the opening paragraph to you once it has been written. This will help identify any errors that need fixing.

6. Begin to write the second and third paragraph using the scaffold provided and support them with ideas or sentence starters.

7. Ask them to think about including a counter argument. This would mean providing an alternative point of view to their own. Use the connectives provided to help guide them.

8. Finally, discuss one of the following options to end their essay or speech:

   - **Ending with a call to action** to try to motivate your audience – 'Let's all do something about this – before it really is too late!'

   - **Ending with a *big* statement** – 'The time has come to end this debate once and for all; mobile phones have no place in the classroom!'

   - **Ending with an appeal to emotions** – 'Today, the future is in our hands and together we can create a better tomorrow.'

Reading non-fiction

Prerequisites, core knowledge or resources

- Features of non-fiction text
- Recap on 'DAFOREST' and language techniques
- Thesauri and dictionaries to look up keywords

In the article below, how does the writer engage the reader? [15 marks]

Hart, A. (2014) 'Generation selfie: Has posing, pouting and posting turned us all into narcissists?', The Telegraph [Online] 5 December, bit.ly/3XbpEIU.

Generation Selfie: Has posing, pouting and posting turned us all into a self-obsessed nation?

"What on earth were you thinking?" I am looking back at my husband's Instagram feed, where a picture of me shivering in a wetsuit stares back at me: hair flat against my face, make-up free, bum blocking the beach. "I was thinking you looked really happy", he says, wounded.

As I try to explain why I'm acting like a celebrity who has just spotted a paparazzo up a tree, how this photo amounts to career suicide, even defamation, I realise that his is, of course, the saner voice. But these days mine is the normal voice. Most women I know would react the same way. In the age of social media and selfies, it's become natural meticulously to police images of ourselves.

I've never thought of myself as high-maintenance — I go make-up free on holidays, can get ready for a night out in under fifteen minutes and never expect to look better than passable — yet I know my good angles. I've perfected a selfie-smile. I have preferred Instagram filters. And I'm not the only one. Vanity has exploded on an epic scale.

---

defamation: insult/abuse
vanity: self-love or obsession
meticulously: attention to detail
epic: huge or large scale

41

Task 1: Can you identify the language features underlined in the article below? Discuss their impact or explain what the writer is trying to say.

Generation Selfie: Has posing, pouting and posting turned us all into a self-obsessed nation?

"What on earth were you thinking?" I am looking back at my husband's Instagram feed,   hair flat
against my face, make-up free, bum blocking the beach.

career suicide, even defamation,
But these days mine is the normal voice.

natural meticulously to police images of ourselves.
I've never thought of myself as high-maintenance — I go make-up free on holidays,

— yet I know my good angles.   a selfie-smile. I
Vanity has exploded on
an epic scale.

Teaching tip: The following are the anticipated pupil responses to the article. Ask the class to begin 'feature spotting' – this will give you an understanding of prior knowledge and will build in some 'quick wins' for the class, particularly for the pupils who are not as confident. Highlight the punctuation as it is visibly identifiable and then lead into discussion around its purpose or function. The writing stems can be used to structure the discussion.

Task 2: Look at the use of punctuation in this article. What is it telling us and why has it been used in certain instances?

Generation Selfie: Has posing, pouting and posting turned us all into a self-obsessed nation?

"What on earth were you thinking?" I am looking back at my husband's Instagram feed, where a picture of me shivering in a wetsuit stares back at me: hair flat against my face, make-up free, bum blocking the beach. "I was thinking you looked really happy", he says, wounded.

As I try to explain why I'm acting like a celebrity who has just spotted a paparazzo up a tree, how this photo amounts to career suicide, even defamation, I realise that his is, of course, the saner voice. But these days mine is the normal voice. Most women I know would react the same way. In the age of social media and selfies, it's become natural meticulously to police images of ourselves.

I've never thought of myself as high-maintenance — I go make-up free on holidays, can get ready fro a night out in under fifteen minutes and never expect to look better than passable — yet I know my good angles. I've perfected a selfie-smile. I have preferred Instagram filters. And I'm not the only one. Vanity has exploded on an epic scale.

On the following page is a sample of pupil responses from teacher-led discussion, ask the class to use the writing frame to construct a response to the question.

Alliterationcombined with a rule of three or triple [plosive sound]

Personal pronoun — aiming the article at 'us' or society or nation

Rule of three again to add comedy and humour to the article — she tells a story for the reader — anecdote. Again, see uses 'bum blocking beach' which is plosive alliteration using the sound the letter 'b' for comic effect — memorable and effective.

Tone change — she becomes more reflective and talks about how she has changed.

She makes her own term of 'selfie-smile'

Rhetorical question — adds to the conversational tone and makes the reader ask themselves the same question. Engages with the reader from the beginning. Who are Generation Selfie?

Generation Selfie: Has posing, pouting and posting turned us all into a self-obsessed nation?

"What on earth were you thinking?" am looking back at my husband's Instagram feed, where a picture of me shivering in a wetsuit stares back at me: hair flat against my face, make-up free, bum blocking the beach. "I was thinking you looked really happy", he says, wounded.

As I try to explain why I'm acting like a celebrity who has just spotted a paparazzo up a tree, how this photo amounts to career suicide, even defamation, I realise that his is, of course, the saner voice. But these days mine is the normal voice. Most women I know react the same way. In the age of social media and selfies, it's become natural meticulously to police images of ourselves.

I've never thought of myself as high-maintenance — I go make-up free on holidays. I can get ready fro a night out in under fifteen minutes and never expect to look better than passable — yet I know my good angles. I've perfected a selfie-smile. I have preferred Instagram filte's. And I'm not the only one. Vanity has exploded on an epic scale.

DAFOREST
Punctuation for effect

Use of the phrase 'career suicide' and 'defamation' are used to exaggerate how bad she thinks the photo of her appears.

'natural meticulously to police' — to pay attention to our photos and 'police' them — in other words check and make sure they are good enough.

Dramatic pause and dash to draw attention to her thoughts and her funny statement about knowing her 'good angles'.

Verb — 'exploded' emphasises how vanity has increased. The adjective 'epic' is used to show how selfies and self obsession have taken over our lives on a huge scale.

In the opening paragraph, the writer uses [TECHNIQUE] when he/she says ... '[EVIDENCE]'		
This tells me ... This tells the reader ... This suggests to the reader that ...	This suggests to the reader that ... This implies that ... This might mean ...	The writer uses this technique because ... ... to reveal to the reader that the writer is... The impact on the reader is that they feel...

Now it's your turn!
Remember to use your notes to guide you.
Take your time and begin with the basics and then build your response by using the tasks.

Sample response to the previous article:
'The writer opens the article with an attention-grabbing headline that includes a rhetorical question combined with alliteration. She says, 'Has posing, pouting and posting turned us all into a self-obsessed nation? The rhetorical question is used to speak directly to the reader. It allows the reader a moment to pause and think about the question and the topic. The alliteration of the verbs 'posing, pouting and posting' make the headline memorable and impactful due to the plosive 'p' sound. She includes the various habits of social media users and how people behave which makes it a relatable headline for many readers.'

'Sweet but Deadly!'

The food giants know that if they added sugar, we buy more. Why? The answer's simple — we're addicted to the deadly sweet stuff! The chairman of the Functional Medicine Institute, Doctor Mark Hyman states that "sugar is more addictive than cocaine"! Professor Simon Capewell from the University of Liverpool has even called sugar, "the new tobacco".

Health chiefs are now telling food manufacturers to slash the amount of sugar they use by at least 30% in order to halt a wave of disaster, disease and death. Obesity already costs the UK over £5 billion a year. Without action, these costs will soar beyond £50 billion by 2050.

So let's be clear — everything from Jelly Babies, Percy Pigs and chocolate bars to biscuits, ice cream and doughnuts need to be an occasional treat and not a daily "fix".

That's the bitter truth about sugar. You have been warned!

Read the article at least twice and complete the tasks.

Task 1: Summarise what the article is about and what the writer is trying to say.

Task 2: In the article, select the three most important sentences and explain why you chose them.

'Sweet but Deadly!'

we buy more. Why?

— we're addicted to the deadly sweet stuff!

"sugar is more addictive than cocaine"!

"the new tobacco".

slash the amount
a wave of disaster, disease and death.

Jelly Babies, Percy Pigs and chocolate bars to biscuits, ice cream and doughnuts need to be an occasional treat and not a daily "fix".

That's the bitter truth about sugar. You have been warned!

Task 3: Use either 'DAFOREST' or your knowledge of parts of speech to highlight the techniques the writer has used. You can create a table of techniques and evidence.

'Sweet but Deadly!'

The food giants know that if they added sugar, we buy more. Why? The answer's simple — we're addicted to the deadly sweet stuff! The chairman of the Functional Medicine Institute, Doctor Mark Hyman states that "sugar is more addictive than cocaine"! Professor Simon Capewell from the University of Liverpool has even called sugar "the new tobacco".

Health chiefs are now telling food manufacturers to slash the amount of sugar they use by at least 30% in order to halt a wave of disaster, disease and death. Obesity already costs the UK over £5 billion a year. Without action, these costs will soar beyond £50 billion by 2050.

So let's be clear — everything from Jelly Babies, Percy Pigs and chocolate bars to biscuits, ice cream and doughnuts need to be an occasional treat and not a daily "fix".

That's the bitter truth about sugar. You have been warned!

Task 4: Can you identify any punctuation for effect? What is the impact of this on the reader?

47

Task 5: What facts, statistics or opinions has the reader used to support their point of view?

Task 6: Now write your full response using the writing frame provided and your own ideas.

In your pairs, decide who will be the **teacher** and who will be the **learner**.
You will use your notes to take the learner through the process step by step.

Explain how the writer has gained and held the interest of the reader.

SELFIE GENERATION LEAVES A BAD TASTE IN MY MOUTH

I've just realised we have entered a new age, one that has changed behaviour, reshaped social structure and — if it goes much further — could threaten the very future of the human race... welcome to the Selfie Age.

I was out for dinner last weekend. Sitting in a Glasgow restaurant, properly excited at my first night out in an eternity, the scene at the next table caught my eye. Four women were all taking photos of their newly-served meals, and then they stared at their phones for the next 10 minutes, presumably uploading the images then checking who'd "liked" their macaroni cheese. However, a quick scan of the room revealed the ladies weren't the only ones plugged into technology.

I admit I'm biased. I can't stand the whole selfie craze. I know exactly what I look like, so I've no need to take 3,425 pics of myself every day!

Low, S. (2016) 'Selfie generation leaves a bad taste in my mouth, says Shari Low', Daily Record [Online] 12 November, bit.ly/3HCc1GS

[CCEA Unit 4: GCSE English Language exam, June 2019 mark scheme]

The text on the following page is the beginning of the article. Explain how the writer engages the interest of the reader.

Explain how the writer engages the interest of the reader.

SHOULD YOU ENCOURAGE YOUR KIDS TO WORK OUT?

Louis is a pro in the gym, and he has the six-pack to show for it. During his weekly workouts, he will start with three rounds of ten press-ups, pull-ups, burpees, jump-rope skips and lifts with a weighted medicine ball to increase his core strength. Nothing wrong with that, you might think — except that Louis is six years old!

A generation ago, playing and running around were the only activities considered necessary to keep children fit and healthy. Now a growing number of national gym chains, including Virgin Active, Better Gyms and David Lloyd, are offering children's memberships to cater to parents panicking about soaring child obesity rates.

According to a new public health report, Britain has the highest obesity rates in Western Europe. One in five children start primary school overweight or obese, rising to more than a third by the time they leave. Increasingly, concerned parents are taking their children with them to the gym.

But is this really a good idea?

Carey, T. (2017) 'Should you encourage your kids to work out?', The Telegraph [Online] 17 November, bit.ly/3YoFk6o.

[CCEA Unit 4: GCSE English Language exam, January 2020 mark scheme]

Using the stages below, ask your partner the following questions and go through the process of breaking down *one* of the articles and write a final response.

1. Ask your partner to define and explain what the features of a non-fiction text are and to provide examples.

2. After reading the selected article at least twice, ask your partner to summarise what it is about and to describe how the writer might be feeling.

3. Ask your partner to explain the different types of language devices they know or recite 'DAFOREST' back to you and explain each language feature as best they can.

4. After reading the article, ask your partner to select what they think are the three most important sentences and explain why they chose them.

5. Now ask them to do some 'feature spotting' by underlining or highlighting the language features in the article. You may wish to create a key.

6. Ask your partner to select examples of punctuation for effect and any facts, opinions, or statistics that they writer has included.

7. Ask your partner to use the writing frame to explain one language feature that the writer has used – they can write it down or tell you their answer verbally.

8. Finally, ask your partner to write three short paragraphs in response to the question 'Explain how the writer engages and/or interests the reader'.

You can prompt them by using the writing frame that follows.

Once you have finished, ask your class teacher to show you the mark scheme and then discuss the points that you could add to your own response. You can also swap roles and use the alternate article provided.

In the opening paragraph, the writer uses [TECHNIQUE] when he/she says ... '[EVIDENCE]'		
This tells me ... *This tells the reader ...* *This suggests that ...*	*This suggests to the reader that ...* *This implies that ...* *This might mean ...*	*The writer uses this technique because ...* *... to reveal to the reader that the writer is...* *The impact on the reader is that they feel...*

Thought stems and useful scaffolds:

opens with a sweeping statement	first person to connect to the reader	use of personal anecdote
a conversational style/ approach	exaggeration is used to develop rapport	short sentences are used to create
metaphor is used by the writer to highlight	use of the rule of three	change in tone

Effective openings

Prerequisites, core knowledge or resources
- What does 'writing for purpose' mean?
- What issues could you be asked to write about?
- How can you engage your target audience?

What is the purpose of each of the following texts?					
newspaper or magazine article	a political party leaflet	a 'How to...' guide	a celebrity's autobiography	a movie or book review	a letter from a charity

entertain	persuade	advise	analyse	argue	describe	explain	inform	instruct

Starter: Read the introductory paragraph and discuss the techniques that the writer has used to engage the reader.*

Example GCSE question

Write an **article** for your **school magazine**, **persuading** the readers to agree with **your views** on the following statement:

"As students we suffer too much stress because of exams."

EXAM CULTURE IS FAILING TEENAGERS!

Is it any wonder that teenagers loathe school? When stress, anxiety and exhaustion are considered 'normal' then we have a problem! Staring at my timetable, I could not help but feel the sudden dread of the long and lonely road that lies ahead. I am constantly thinking about how I am going to cope. What will be left of us once the marathon of exams chews us up and spits us out? There must be a better way – there has to be – otherwise school life will continue to be miserable for millions of teenagers.

Follow-up questions:

1. Is this an effective opening? Explain your answer.
2. How do you think the writer feels? Explain your answer.
3. What could you do to improve it?
4. How would you begin the next paragraph?

*This table will give you some ideas for labelling the article:

conversational style	rhetorical question	triples	punctuation for effect
alliteration	metaphor	emotive language	pun

DO

Now it's your turn!
Remember to use your notes to guide you.
Take your time and begin with the basics and then build your writing gradually.

Writing task: Using the cue cards in the following table, construct an effective and engaging opening.

Write an article for your school magazine persuading the readers to agree with your views on the following statement:

"Bullying in schools is a major issue and it needs to be addressed!"

or

"Uniforms are unnecessary and we shouldn't be forced to wear them."

Don't you think that...?	Is it any wonder that...?	Have you ever thought about ...?
Can you imagine...?	Are you fed up with...?	How can we continue to...?
degrading	miserable	unpleasant
incredible	thrilled	precious
Can you include a metaphor?	Can you include alliteration?	Can you use punctuation for effect?

In your pairs, decide who will be the **teacher** and who will be the **learner**. You will use your notes to take the learner through the process step by step.

1. What does '**writing for purpose**' mean?
    - Name a text that advises
    - Name a text that entertains
    - Name a text that instructs

2. Can you write **one** example of the following techniques:
    - Personal pronouns
    - Rhetorical questions
    - Triples
    - Alliteration
    - Metaphor

3. Read the following question and write the opening:

    > Write a **speech** for your **classmates**, **persuading** them to agree with **your views** on the following statement:
    >
    > *"We are all responsible for looking after the environment."*

4. Give the learner 15-20 minutes to plan, write and review their opening to the above statement. You can prompt them using the cue cards or recommend techniques.

5. Once the learner has completed the task, ask them to read it aloud like a speech and then read it back to them so they can hear it too.

6. Now you will **assess** the learners opening using the checklist. Have they included any of the following:
    - a direct address to the audience   [1 mark]
    - a triple or a rule of three   [2 marks]
    - emotive language   [2 marks]

TEACH

- alliteration   [2 marks]
- a rhetorical question   [3 marks]
- an effective metaphor   [3 marks]
- a conversational style   [3 marks]
- punctuation for effect   [3 marks]

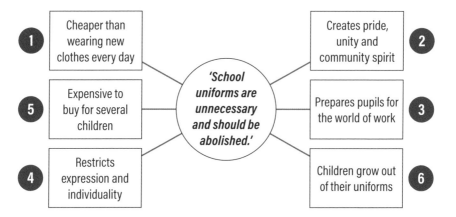
Speaking and listening: shaping talk

Prerequisites, core knowledge or resources

- Practise framing discussion using the scaffolds provided
- Mini whiteboards can be used to record responses
- Awareness of the topics below or research beforehand

> 'School uniforms are unnecessary and should be abolished.'
>
> 'Phones have no place in schools and should be banned!'
>
> 'Social media should only be available for over-18s.'
>
> 'Female sports stars should be paid the same as males.'
>
> 'Zoos are cruel – all animals should be released into the wild.'
>
> 'Computer games and movies encourage violence!'

Task 1: Draw a spider diagram and begin to record your thoughts, reactions and responses to one of the statements above.

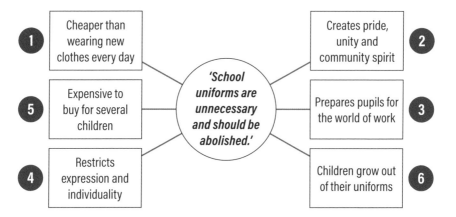

1. Cheaper than wearing new clothes every day
2. Creates pride, unity and community spirit
5. Expensive to buy for several children
3. Prepares pupils for the world of work
4. Restricts expression and individuality
6. Children grow out of their uniforms

'School uniforms are unnecessary and should be abolished.'

Task 2: Begin to **label your ideas** in terms strength of argument.

(For example: 1 being the strongest argument or point and then 5 being the least important point or argument.)

Task 3: Create a **for** and **against** table for your chosen statement. Try and incorporate the word 'because' in your table to help you.

School uniforms are **necessary and should remain because...**	School uniforms are **unnecessary and should be abolished because...**

Task 4: Get into groups or pairs and begin to discuss each of your points using the prompt card and scaffolds provided.

'In my opinion...' 'In my view...'	'I believe...' 'I strongly believe ...'	'I agree with [name] because...'	'I disagree with [name] because...'
'I understand your point of view, but what about...'	'But what if...?' 'But what about...?'	Why do you think...? For what reason ...?	'To summarise, as a group, we think that...'
Can you include any connectives when making your points?			

DO

Now it's your turn!
Remember to use your notes to guide you.
Take your time and begin with the basics and then build your writing gradually.

Task 1: In your groups or in pairs, discuss the following topic:

'Young people are addicted to technology and social media.'

Task 2: Draw a spider diagram and begin to record your thoughts, reactions, and responses to the statement above.

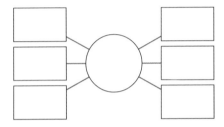

Task 2: Begin to label your ideas in terms strength of argument.

Task 3: Create a **for** and **against** table for your chosen statement. Try and incorporate the word 'because' in your table to help you.

*I **agree** that young people are addicted to technology and social media **because**...*	*I **disagree** that young people are addicted to technology and social media **because**...*

Task 4: Get into groups or pairs and begin to discuss each of your points using the prompt card and scaffolds below.

Can you use the following discursive markers to shape your points?

'In my opinion...' *'In my view...'*	*'I believe...'* *'I strongly believe ...'*	*'I agree with [name] because...'*	*'I disagree with [name] because...'*
'I understand your point of view, but what about...'	*'But what if...?'* *'But what about...?'*	*Why do you think...?* *For what reason ...?*	*'To summarise, as a group, we think that...'*

In your pairs, decide who will be the **teacher** and who will be the **learner.**
You will use your notes to take the learner through the process step by step.

Select **one** of the titles below OR **come up with one of your own**:

> *'Phones have no place in schools and should be banned!'*
>
> *'Social media should only be available to over-18s.'*
>
> *'Female sports stars should be paid the same males.'*
>
> *'Zoos are cruel - all animals should be released into the wild.'*
>
> *'Computer games and movies encourage violence!'*

1. Ask the learner to discuss their views on the topic with you informally and record some of their ideas.

2. Ask the learner to record their thoughts, responses and ideas using a spider diagram structure.

3. Ask the learner to put their arguments or points in order of importance and explain their reasoning.

4. After they have organised their arguments, place them into a 'For and Against' table and ask them to elaborate on each of their points.

5. Ask the learner to begin to share their thoughts and arguments by using the prompts and scaffolds to structure their talk. You can challenge them on their views and ask them to elaborate.

Shaping talk: sharing your views

'In my opinion...' 'In my view...'	'I believe...' 'I strongly believe ...'	'I agree with [name] because...'	'I disagree with [name] because...'
'I understand your point of view, but what about...'	'But what if...?' 'But what about...?'	Why do you think...? For what reason ...?	'To summarise, as a group, we think that...'
Can you include any **connectives** *when making your points?*			

Shaping talk: structuring your thoughts

To begin with, ...	Firstly ... Secondly ... Again, ...	Apart from ...	In summary, ...
It is clear that...	Next, ... Without doubt, ...	On the other hand, ...	To conclude, ...
It is undeniable that...	The most compelling reason is that ...	However, ...	Ultimately, ...

Creative writing

Assessment objectives   **[CCEA: Writing AO4]**

- Communicate clearly, effectively and imaginatively.
- Organise information and ideas into structured and sequenced
- Use a range of sentence structures for clarity, purpose and effect, with accurate spelling, punctuation and grammar.

Create a spider diagram describing what you can see.

Zoom in and focus on different parts of the image

Task 1: Write your immediate thoughts, descriptions and ideas about the image.

Task 2: As a class, label the image with ideas, thoughts and suggestions.

Task 3: Use the 5Ws and 5 senses to develop ideas around the image. *What is happening? Where is it? Who is the character in the image? How did the character get there? Can you predict what will happen next?*

Task 4: Zoom in and focus on certain sections of the image and describe them in close detail. Use descriptive vocabulary and language techniques to extend your ideas.

Task 5: Read the pupil responses below then use them to discuss 'writer's craft'.

[You can introduce this at the start or end of this lesson.]

Pupil example 1:

I walked to the edge of the river. I stood looking at the house. It was lit up by a dull, yellow light. I saw an owl in the tree and some fireflies in the air. Maybe I should wait until morning. Will it be safer to walk across the swamp when it is bright?

Pupil example 2:

Carefully, I crept to the edge of the sweltering, spongy swamp. From a safe distance, I studied the abandoned, stilted shack. It stood above the water like a beacon in the dark with its blurry yellow lights that flickered through the tiny arched windows. An owl was perched on a thick branch above as if keeping watch over the area, ready to alert the inhabitants of the presence of invaders. Fireflies hung in the air like seeker drones over the surface of the water. Perhaps I should wait for daylight. Or do I take my chances, slim as they are, and try to reach the muddy bank opposite?

Assessment objectives   [CCEA: Writing AO4]

- Communicate clearly, effectively and imaginatively.
- Organise information and ideas into structured and sequenced
- Use a range of sentence structures for clarity, purpose and effect, with accurate spelling, punctuation and grammar.

Create a spider diagram describing what you can see.

Zoom in and focus on different parts of the image

Task 1: Write your immediate thoughts, descriptions and ideas about the image.

Create a spider diagram or stick the image onto the centre of your page and write some ideas around it. Describe what you see and what might be happening.

Task 2: Use the 5 Ws and 5 senses to develop ideas around the image.

What is happening? Where is it? Who is the character in the image?

How did the character get there? Can you predict what will happen next?

Could you use analepsis or prolepsis?

Task 3: Zoom in and focus on certain sections of the image and describe them in close detail. Use descriptive vocabulary and language techniques to extend your ideas.

You can use the 'slow writing' frame below to enhance your opening:

- *Sentence **one** must describe using the **senses***
- *Sentence **two** must use **exactly five words***
- *Sentence **three** must begin with an **adverb***
- *Sentence **four** must be a **rhetorical question***
- *Sentence **five** must be a **metaphor** or **simile***
- *Sentence **six** must include an **exclamation [!]**, **rhetorical question [?] or ellipsis […]***

You can rearrange the sentences in the order that you think works best for you.

Suggested opener:

'*Standing by the shore, he watched the boats come in one by one…*'

'*She saw him waiting for her, it had been 20 years since…*'

Assessment objectives   **[CCEA: Writing AO4]**

- Communicate clearly, effectively and imaginatively.
- Organise information and ideas into structured and sequenced
- Use a range of sentence structures for clarity, purpose and effect, with accurate spelling, punctuation and grammar.

Create a spider diagram describing what you can see.

1. Set a timer for **10 minutes**. Ask the learner to note down their immediate thoughts and ideas using the 5 senses and 5 Ws.

2. Ask the learner to **circle three areas** of the image that they will **zoom in** on and use as the **focus** of their writing.

3. Ask them to use the **writing frame** and **provide prompts** or **ideas** for them. They can use a word bank or thesaurus to enhance their writing.

- *Sentence **one** must describe using the **senses***
- *Sentence **two** must use **exactly five words***

- *Sentence **three** must begin with an **adverb***
- *Sentence **four** must be a **rhetorical question***
- *Sentence **five** must be a **metaphor** or **simile***
- *Sentence **six** must include an **exclamation [!]**, **rhetorical question [?] or ellipsis [...]***

The learner can **rearrange** the sentences in the order that works best for them. Use them as a prompt to support their writing.

Reading media texts

Assessment objectives: **[CCEA AO3: Writing]**

- Read and understand texts, selecting material appropriate to purpose.
- Develop and sustain interpretations of writers' ideas and perspectives.
- Explain and evaluate how writers use linguistic, structural and presentational features to achieve effects and engage and influence the reader.

Task 4 and Task 5 of Unit 1 are **connected**. They are both **media texts**.

In Task 4, you will get a short piece of text related to the image that follows in Task 5.

Task 4 can also aid your understanding and response in Task 5 and vice versa.

Read the text below. Explain how language has been used to promote this as an exciting experience. Present evidence to support your comments.

Did you know that Northern Ireland is the most important location for the epic series, "Game of Thrones"? We think this was an inspired choice. The Northern Ireland sets, landscapes and castles all look fantastic on screen!

Our "Game of Thrones" tour is nothing like most sightseeing coach tours. As well as visiting the renowned Giant's Causeway, we will take you on exciting location treks so that you can explore the stunning and now famous locations used in the series.

Discover Dunluce Castle, the 17th century ruins that were used as the exterior of the House of Greyjoy; pose for pictures at Ballintoy Harbour, the location of many classic scenes but ... will you have the courage to cross Carrick-a-Redge Rope Bridge? Our final stop will be the iconic Dark Hedges with it's spectacular archway of intertwined trees, the setting for the escape of Ayra and Gendry from King's Landing.

We also offer a unique and fun "immersive experience", as we have costumes, swords and shields on the coach for everybody to use — at no extra cost.

Whether you are a "Game of Thrones" fan or not, this really is the ultimate North Coast experience!

Adapted from GAMEOFTHRONESTOURS.COM

Task 1: What do you think the word '**promote**' means? Can you think of any synonyms for the word 'promote'?

Task 2: Read the extract carefully. Label and highlight any key words and phrases, language techniques or sentences that you think are important.

Task 3: Write down **three reasons** why you think this would be an **exciting** experience for tourists. Look up the following words: epic, renowned, iconic, intertwined and immersive.

Task 4: Read the pupil example and discuss the **features of a good response**.

> From the outset, the advert uses a rhetorical question that directly appeals to tourists wishing to see parts of Northern Ireland: "Did you know...most important location... epic series, "Game of Thrones?" It includes the word "epic" implying that, like the series, this tour is impressive and extraordinary.
>
> The advert includes positive language such as "inspired choice" and "fantastic on screen" to promote what Northern Ireland has to offer tourists and creates a sense of hyperbole. This is further emphasised by the use of the exclamatory statements.
>
> The choice of positive adjectives such as "renowned", "stunning" and "iconic" helps to develop a sense of enthusiasm by praising the variety of sightseeing locations on the tour.

Task 5: Can you write **two more good paragraphs** to add to the sample response?

Select two examples of presentational features from the cover.

Explain the intended effect of each of these two presentational features.

Pro tip: Most images can be split into thirds – try this to focus on certain features.

The eye catching image of the...
The dominant central image of...
Tagline or review suggests...
The use of contrasting colours suggests...
The colours _____ and _____ dominate which reflect the setting/genre/mood/ atmosphere.

© Game of Thrones Tours Ltd

You are being asked to select specific **presentational fixtures** such as **image**, **colour**, **layout** and **font**. You must then **explain** why you think the poster, leaflet or cover has been designed a particular way and the effect.

Task 1: What can you see in the image? Think about the **images**, **colours** and **layout** and write a brief comment on them.

Task 2: What is the effect of this flyer on the person who is **buying the product** or thinking of **visiting the attraction**?

Task 3: How would it sway or persuade them to pay for the product, activity or experience?

Presentational features could include the following:

- The title size, colour and placement and use of font.
- Image of the armoured figure and how it is positioned.
- Image of the castle, sunset and the shoreline.
- Tagline and where it is placed.

Task 4: Read the pupil example and discuss the **features of a good response**.

> *The grey coloured title is large and is eye-catching and placed at the top. The dominant central image of the armoured arms and shield creates a central focus and is striking. This relates to the show Game of Thrones and will attract fans of the show as they will be familiar with it.*
>
> *The colours are dramatic and the images of the castle and the red sky creates a sense of adventure and evokes a feeling of drama and or a quest. The tagline is used to show where more information can be found and is printed in white to catch the eye of the reader.*

Task 5: Can you add any more points about image, colour and layout?

Assessment objectives   [CCEA AO3: Writing]

- Read and understand texts, selecting material appropriate to purpose.
- Develop and sustain interpretations of writers' ideas and perspectives.
- Explain and evaluate how writers use linguistic, structural and presentational features to achieve effects and engage and influence the reader.

Question: Read the text below. Explain how language has been used to promote Titanic Belfast as a venue for hire. Present evidence to support your comments.

> Titanic Belfast is an iconic building that offers spectacular conference and banqueting facilities in an array of architecturally distinct spaces.
>
> Located on the top floors of Titanic Belfast with stunning views of the Slipways and Belfast Lough, where the world-famous liner was designed, built and launched, the Titanic Suites offer clients enormous flexibility.
>
> With capacity for intimate dinner parties of 20 to large-scale receptions for 1,500 – the possibilities for your conference, banquet, exhibition or wedding reception are endless!
>
> The opulent decor in the Titanic Suites is themed on the interiors of Titanic and features a stunning replica of the liner's famous Grand Staircase.
>
>   **titanicbelfast.com**

Task 1: Read the extract carefully. Label and highlight any key words and phrases, language techniques or sentences that you think are important.

Task 2: Write down **three reasons** why you think this would be a good place to have an event such as a wedding or conference.

Task 3: Look up the following words: distinct, intimate, capacity, opulent and replica.

Task 4: Using the structure on the following page, begin to write your response to the question.

From the outset, the advert _____ .

The advert might be appealing to _____ .

It includes the word(s) "_____" implying _____ .

The advert includes positive language such as _____ to promote.

This is further emphasised by the use of _____ .

The main selling point is _____ because _____ .

The choice of positive adjectives such as _____ , _____ and

_____ .

Aims to develop a sense of _____ by praising the variety

of _____ the venue has to offer.

It also includes interesting points such as _____ in order to

_____ .

Select two examples of presentational features from the cover below. Explain the intended effect of each of these two presentational features.

Pro tip: Most images can be split into thirds — try this to focus on certain features.

The eye catching image of the...

The dominant central image of...

Tagline or review suggests...

The use of contrasting colours suggests...

You are being asked to select specific **presentational fixtures** such as **image**, **colour**, **layout** and **font**. You must then **explain** why you think the poster, leaflet or cover has been designed a particular way and its intended effect.

Task 1: What can you see in the image? Think about the **images**, **colours** and **layout** and write a brief comment on them.

Task 2: What is the effect of this flyer on the person who is **buying the product** or thinking of **visiting the attraction?**

Task 3: How would it sway or persuade them to pay for the product, activity or experience?

Task 4: List the presentational features such as image, colour and layout.

> The _____ is large and is eye-catching and placed _____ .
>
> The dominant central image of the _____ and _____ creates a central focus and is striking. This relates to the _____ and will attract people to the venue.
>
> The colours such as _____ are dramatic and _____ .
>
> The images of the _____ and the _____ creates a sense of _____ and evokes a feeling of _____ .
>
> The tagline is used to _____ and is printed in _____ to catch the eye and _____ .

 **TEACH** Reading media texts

Assessment objectives [CCEA AO3: Writing]
- Read and understand texts, selecting material appropriate to purpose.
- Develop and sustain interpretations of writers' ideas and perspectives.
- Explain and evaluate how writers use linguistic, structural and presentational features to achieve effects and engage and influence the reader.

Read the text below. Explain how language has been used to promote the Giant's Causeway as a tourist attraction. Present evidence to support your comments.

> Planning a day out to the North Coast? No trip would be complete without a visit to the world-famous Giant's Causeway. As Northern Ireland's only UNESCO World Heritage Site, this must-see place has many must-see sights.
>
> The Grand Causeway is the largest of three rock outcrops which make up the Giant's Causeway. These collections of curious columns contributed to the causeway being designated Northern Ireland's only World Heritage Site by UNESCO in 1986.
>
> Experience a bird's eye view of the Giant's Causeway with the clifftop trails. Boasting undiscovered views, it's a unique way to see the World Heritage Site and explore the stunning north coast of Ireland. With a red, blue, green and yellow trail, there's a route for every ability.
>
> Officially opened in July 2012, the Giant's Causeway Visitor Centre has won many prestigious awards for design innovation and sustainability. Having racked up your step count on the trails, the cafe is the perfect place to enjoy a tasty treat and the shop is an ideal location to pick up a souvenir of your bucket list visit.

1. **Set a timer for eight minutes and ask the learner to read the extract carefully.**

   They must label and highlight any key words and phrases, language techniques or sentences that you think are important.

2. **Ask the learner to** write down **three reasons** why you think this would be a good place to visit

3. **Ask the learner to look up the following words:** outcrops; curious; prestigious; innovation and sustainability – and write their definitions.

4. **Using the structure below**, ask them to write their response to the question.

From the outset, the advert _____ .

The advert might be appealing to _____ .

It includes the word(s) "_____" implying _____ .

The advert includes positive language such as _____ to promote.

This is further emphasised by the use of _____ .

The main selling point is _____ because

_____ .

The choice of positive adjectives such as _____, _____ and

_____ .

Aims to develop a sense of _____ by praising the variety of _____ the venue has to offer.

It also includes interesting points such as _____ in order to

_____ .

Select two examples of presentational features from the graphic below. Explain the intended effect of each of these two presentational features.

© Content Kings Media Ltd

5. **Ask the learner to list the presentational features such as image, colour and layout in relation to the website.**

6. **What can you see in the image?** Think about the **images, colours** and **layout** and write a brief comment on them.

7. **What is the effect of this website on the person** who is **buying the product** or thinking of **visiting the attraction?**

8. **How would it sway or persuade them** to pay for the product, activity or experience? How does the website layout encourage the user to find out more?

9. **List the presentational features such as image, colour and layout.**

10. **Using the structure below,** ask them to write their response to the question.

The _____ is large and is eye-catching and placed _____ .
The dominant central image of the _____ and _____ creates a central focus and is striking. This relates to the _____ and will attract people to the venue.
The colours such as _____ are dramatic and _____ .
The images of the _____ and the _____ creates a sense of _____ and evokes a feeling of _____ .
The tagline is used to _____ and is printed in _____ to catch the eye and _____ .

Literary comparatives

Prerequisites, core knowledge or resources
- Review the 'writer's craft'
- Using comparative connectives
- Embedding evidence in your analysis

Consider text A and B from the English Language Unit 4 June 2022 exam paper:

<u>Compare and contrast</u> how the writers have <u>**created a sense of unease**</u> in their writing. Present supporting evidence from both texts.

Task 1: Spend **8 minutes** reading the extracts from the **CCEA 2022 Unit 4 exam**.

Task 2: Begin to **label and highlight** the **language techniques** and writer's choice of words in each extract. Can you identify any themes or links between the language in each extract? As a class, can you use a Venn diagram to compare the two texts?

Task 3: Read the pupil example and discuss the **features of a good response**.

SEE Literary comparatives

'In both texts, there is a sense of fear and uncertainty for the main characters. The opening of both texts also includes the use of short impactful sentences. Text A uses one-word sentences to create mystery around the central character. Likewise, text B uses one-word sentences to create tension and an uncertain atmosphere. For example, 'Roy, 'Footsteps' 'Running', 'Faster' and 'Stronger'. This conveys a sense of immediate threat and unease in the reader.

In text B, the writer uses personification 'shadows danced...stared' to create unease as if the environment is reacting to the situation. When combined with the adverb 'densely' overcast, a dark and ominous atmosphere are created. Meanwhile, text A makes effective use of punctuation by including ellipsis, 'fifteen...fourteen...thirteen...' to give the impression of a countdown whilst developing tension and suspense. This reinforces the sense of unease as it helps to develop and build the dramatic plot.'

	Structuring your answer	
In text A/B, the writer uses the adjective/ action verbs/adverbs... to describe... to emphasise... to convey... to capture the feeling of... gives the impression of ...	**Connectives and openers:** It is clear from the beginning that... In both texts ... However, ... Likewise, ... On the other hand, ...	**Ending:** Overall, both texts create a sense of ... I feel that text A/B is more successful because... Overall, both texts deal with the themes of

DO

Prerequisites, core knowledge or resources

- Review the 'writer's craft'
- Using comparative connectives
- Embedding evidence in your analysis

Consider text A and B from the English Language Unit 4 June 2021 exam paper:

To help understanding for the key terms of question, explore synonyms and alternative vocabulary.			
Q. Compare and contrast how the writers of text A and B have created a sense of tension/mystery/suspense [see 'suspense' mnemonic in appendix].			
nervous	fearful	on-edge	strained
uptight	nail-biting	hostility	apprehension

Q. Compare and contrast how the writers of text A and B have created a tense atmosphere.			
setting	mood	feeling	tone
undercurrent	impression	conditions	semblance

<u>**Compare and contrast**</u> how the writers of text A and text B have **created a sense of a threatening situation** for their readers. Present supporting evidence from both texts.

Narrator: Who is telling the story and what is the point of view?

- Is a character telling the story?

- Is it written in the first, second or third person?

Opening: How does each extract begin?

- Does it begin with a dramatic opening? Do any words stand out?
- Can you spot <u>one</u> language device that the writer has used?
- Do any words or phrases suggest anything about the story [adjective/verbs/adverbs]?

Character: How is the character described? How are they feeling?

- Does it mention the **character's appearance**?
- How do they behave or **how do they feel**? [adverbs – *ly* words]
- **How do you think they are feeling and how do you know?**

Setting: How does the writer describe the setting?

- Both texts use **descriptive details** to create a sense of … [think about the mood]
- **Does the writer use any language devices** [similes/metaphors/rule of three/listing]?
- How does it add **tension/suspense/mystery**? [How does the reader feel or react?]
- What **particular words** or **phrases** do they use [strong adjective/verbs/adverbs]?

Sentences: Can you spot any short paragraphs or sentences?

- Do both texts use **short paragraphs** to heighten the dramatic effect?
- Do both texts use **short abrupt sentences** to create a dramatic, tense moment in the passage?
- Can you spot any **punctuation for effect** in both texts? [… ! ? –]

Ending: How does the extract end?

- Text A/B **ends dramatically** with… [… ! ?]   I feel that text A/B is more successful because…

DO

Structuring your answer		
In text A/B, the writer uses the adjective/ action verbs/adverbs...	**Connectives and openers:**	**Ending:**
to describe...	*It is clear from the beginning that...*	*Overall, both texts create a sense of ...*
to emphasise...	*In both texts ...*	*I feel that text A/B is more successful because...*
to convey...	*However, ...*	*Overall, both texts deal with the themes of*
to capture the feeling of...	*Likewise, ...*	
gives the impression of ...	*On the other hand, ...*	

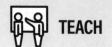

Prerequisites, core knowledge or resources
- Review the 'writer's craft'
- Using comparative connectives
- Embedding evidence in your analysis

Consider text A and B from the English Language Unit 4 June 2019 exam paper:

To help understanding for the key terms of question, explore synonyms and alternative vocabulary.			
Q. Compare and contrast how the writers of text A and B have created a sense of tension/mystery/suspense [see 'suspense' mnemonic in appendix].			
nervous	fearful	on-edge	strained
uptight	nail-biting	hostility	apprehension

Q. Compare and contrast how the writers of text A and B have created a tense atmosphere.			
setting	mood	feeling	tone
undercurrent	impression	conditions	semblance

Compare and contrast how the writers of texts A and B have **created a tense atmosphere**. Present supporting evidence from both texts.

1. Set a timer for 8 minutes and ask the learner to read both extracts. In that time, they must label key language techniques, identify key words and the most important sentences in each text.

2. Ask them to describe to you what is happening in each extract and explain their reasons for selecting parts of the text. Remind the learner to refer to the key terms of the question in their response.

3. Ask the learner to place their initial thoughts and ideas into a table or Venn diagram in order to identify similarities and differences between each text. Remind them to consider the shared themes.

4. Ask the learner to begin to write their response. Use the scaffolds provided in the previous lessons and the additional prompts below. You can both consult the mark scheme to check the quality of your answer and discuss improvements.

Additional prompts

- 'Both texts use **descriptive details** to create a sense of ...'
- 'Both texts use **short or single line paragraphs** to heighten the dramatic effect for example, ...'
- '**Short sentences** are used to create a dramatic, tense moment in the passage for example, ...'
- 'The passage **ends dramatically** with ...'

Key terms

What is scaffolding?

Effect size 0.82

Scaffolding is to simplify a task and make it more manageable by providing temporary supportive steps along the way. It provides direction to help pupils focus on achieving a goal. It will reduce frustration and, by modelling what we want to achieve, we create clearly defined expectations. Scaffolding provides the support in the early stage of writing and it is then removed when it is no longer required once a high degree of success is evident. It can motivate pupils and develop their independent writing skills. Scaffolds can help create a classroom environment that nurtures students rather than merely correcting their mistakes.[1]

How can I build it into my lessons?

- Provide sentence stems, starters or writing frames.
- Model examples by showing how it is done and talk it through.
- Bitesize or chunk the writing task and model each step.
- Use connectives or discursive markers to aid structuring or paragraphing.
- Provide word banks and topic specific vocabulary.
- Create a support sheet with key words related to the topic for SEND and CA.
- Create visual scaffolds by dividing space on the page or including image prompts.

What is deliberate practice?

Effect size 0.79

---

1   Hasan, B. A. (2001). The Relationship of Writing Apprehension and Self-Esteem to the Writing Quality and Quantity of EFL University Students. ERIC. (Report). bit. ly/3xGdszs.

 **KEY TERMS** Key terms

Deliberate practice focuses on skill improvement by using small, incremental steps. It is purposeful and systematic which makes it focused and requires full attention[2]. It is a method of breaking down the task and focusing on the essential elements for improvement, providing feedback and then revisiting to ensure the skill is embedded.

How can I build it into my lessons?

- **Isolate** the skill that you want to improve and explain why it is important.
- **Develop** the skill by revisiting the rules, providing support and guidance along the way.
- **Assess** the skill to make sure the pupil's knowledge and skill is competent and secure.
- **Perform** the skill by completing the task again either individually or as a group.
- **Practise** at another point in time and continue to revisit until automaticity is achieved.

What is feedback?

Effect size 0.73

Research suggests positive feedback is specific, accurate and clear. Feedback is used to improve the student's learning and redirects or refocuses the actions of teacher and student so there is a clear outcome to achieving a goal. It can be oral or written, formative or summative. Feedback should always be specific advice a student can use to improve their performance. There is evidence that feedback is more effective if it focuses on the task, not the person, and that feedback on familiar tasks has more impact[3]. Normalising error helps promote a culture of actionable feedback and self-improvement.

---

2 Anders Ericsson, A., Krampe, R. T. and Tesch-Romer, C. (1993). The Role of Deliberate Practice in the Acquisition of Expert Performance, *Psychological Review*, 100(3), 363–406.

3 Kluger, A. N. and DeNisi, A. (1996). The effects of feedback interventions on performance: A historical review, a meta-analysis, and a preliminary feedback intervention theory, *Psychological Bulletin*, 119(2), 254–284.

How can I build it into my lessons?

- Make sure it is goal referenced – you could link it to specifics within a success criteria.

- Make it actionable so they know what to do and explain the process using clear steps.

- Make it timely – it is most valuable when it is given immediately following the task.

- It needs to be consistent, accurate and stable – use a format that is pupil friendly like a cover sheet.

- Feedback can be varied using either whole class feedback or personalised individual feedback.

- Use self or peer review to develop a student's capacity to evaluate their own work or the work of others.

Using mnemonics and dual coding

Pupils often struggle to spell the word rhetorical correctly and can find it difficult to identify what the question is doing or will often feature spot and not mention the effect of the technique. This mnemonic might help them remember how to spell and how to explain the effect. You could turn this into a simple cloze passage or fill in the blanks after they have learned the bullet points – or even turn it into a wall display!

Rhetorical questions:

- **raise** doubt
- **helps emphasise** specific points
- make the reader **think**
- may have an **obvious** answer
- capture **readers interest**
- **challenge** the listener or reader
- grab the **attention** of the **listener** or reader

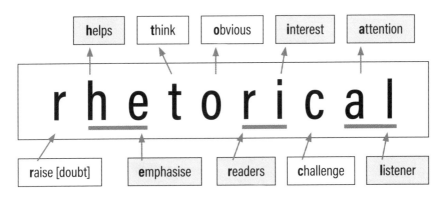

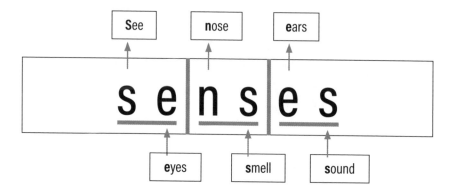

This is particularly good for juniors as you can include the actions. There is a variation of spelling of this word every year and this is one method I have used to help correct it. When they are writing about setting, it can also be used as a prompt to include sensory imagery.

Repetition is another word that is commonly misspelt and can be tricky. The interesting thing is that the word does the very thing that it is referring to – the letters within the word are repeated. When we discuss this, I ask the class to tell me what is happening in the word and then they have the definition. You can then do a quick fill in the blanks to reinforce the spelling. I had an excellent French teacher who used the commands *répétez s'il vous plait* or *répète après moi* and this also helped me identify the spelling of the word. Exploit the cross overs, spelling patterns or the etymology!

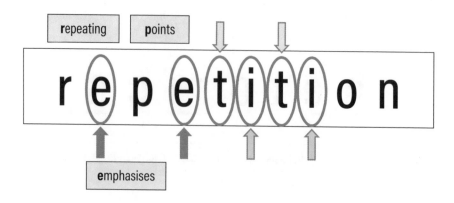

r _ p _ t _ t _ o n

Again, using the shortened version of the word can help pupils remember the effect of statistics. It is a tricky word to spell but in an exam the word stats can also be substituted. They can also act as sentence stems or starters when coupled with a piece of non-fiction or a speech.

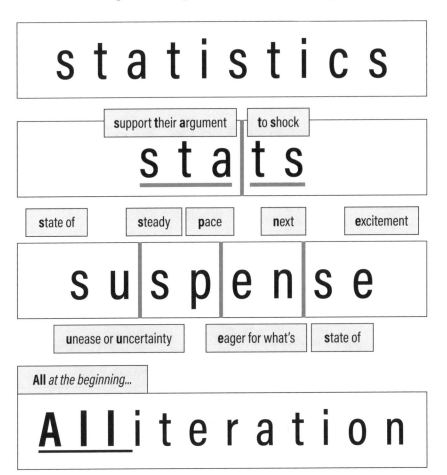

The occurrence of the **same letter or sound at the beginning** of adjacent or closely connected words.

If *an object was a* **person...**

the attribution of a personal nature or human characteristics to something <u>non-human</u>, or the representation of an abstract quality in human form.

Begins with an 's' - the clue is in the name as the sound features at the beginning!
s i b i l a n c e

Sibilance is a literary device and figure of speech wherein a hissing sound is created in a group of words through the repetition of 's' sounds.

Begins with an 'a' - the clue is in the name as it begins with a vowel!
a s s o n a n c e

Begins with an 'c' - the clue is in the name as it begins with a consonant!
c o n s o n a n c e